Dear Dr. Fisch

Children's Letters
to a
Holocaust Survivor

Dear Dr. Fisch

Children's Letters
to a
Holocaust Survivor

By Robert O. Fisch and hundreds of tomorrow's leaders

Editing and letter selection by Kathleen Cleberg

Illustrations by Robert O. Fisch

Nodin Press

ISBN 1-932472-08-8

Nodin Press, a division of Micawbers, Inc.
530 N. Third Street,
Suite 120
Minneapolis, MN 55401

I want to thank all the students and teachers of the schools I visited. Each of your letters was beautiful and, taken together, they were the most rewarding experience of my life.

Opening each letter was a thrill and reading its contents a delight. The response to the horrifying loss of millions became the creative seed for beauty, compassion and appreciation of freedom. I want to share some with you. I couldn't make the selection. I am biased and each of them is so dear to me. I asked my friend Kathleen Cleberg to do that.

I hope the young generations will come to live in a better world, where humanity overcomes hatred. This will not take place by wishful thinking but by education, compassion, love and hard work by young people, their parents, their teachers and society as well.

Tormented by the memory of the past
Being in hell, where the living were burned alive
Now I am free, begging on my knees
Use my blood, for love.

written after the liberation in 1945

R. O. F.

List of Schools

Academy of Holy Angels, Richfield MN
Battle Creek Middle School, St. Paul MN
Blessed Trinity, Richfield MN
Burnsville High School Senior Campus, Burnsville MN
Cambridge High School, Cambridge MN
Central High School, St Paul MN
Central Middle School, Eden Prairie MN
Cleveland Middle School, St. Paul MN
Fred Moore Middle Junior and Secondary School, Anoka MN
Fridley High School, Fridley MN
Gunskirchen High School, Austria
Gustavus Adolfus College, St. Peter MN
Hazel Park Academy, St. Paul MN
Hildburghause High School, Germany
Holdingford High School, MN
Homecraft Elementary School, St. Paul MN
Lake County School, Minneapolis MN
Lake Harriet Community School, Minneapolis MN
Middle School of Eden Prairie MN
Minnehaha Academy, Minneapolis MN
Morristown High School, Morristown NJ
Ogilvie High School, Ogilvie MN
Orono Middle School, Orono MN
Our Lady of Grace, Edina MN
Pine City High School, Pine City MN
Pine Bluff High School, AR
Pulaski Heights Junior High School, Little Rock AR

Radnoti Gymnasium, Budapest Hungary
Ramsey Junior High School, St. Paul MN
Redwing High School, Redwing MN
Richfield Middle School, Richfield MN
Robbinsdale High School, Robbinsdale, MN
Roseville Area Middle School, Little Canada MN
Sauk Center High School, Sauk Center MN
Scott Highland Middle School, Apple Valley MN
Shakopee Junior High School, Minneapolis MN
Simley High School, Inner Grove Heights MN
South High School, Eagan MN
South High School, Minneapolis MN
St. Croix Valley High School, St. Croix MN
St. Joseph Catholic Junior High School, Pine Bluff AR
St. Louis Park Junior High, Minneapolis MN
St. Paul Academy, St. Paul MN
St. Peter's Catholic Elementary School, St. Paul MN
St. Peter High School, St. Peter MN
St. Rose of Lima, Roseville MN
The Central Public School, Norwood MN
Youth Initiative, Minneapolis MN
University of Klagenfurt, Austria
University St. Thomas, St. Paul MN
Waconia High School, Waconia MN
Watson Park, Richey FL
Wayzata West Middle School, Wayzata MN

Introduction

To me the Holocaust was never a subject for conversation.

How did it happen, then, that it became something I talk about over and over again? In 1989 I offered to design cover illustrations for *Minnesota Medicine* magazine. I was told they needed a Holocaust illustration for an article about an ethics meeting discussing the use of experiments from Nazi concentration camps.

I thought for a long time. Who could artistically express the magnitude of human suffering and the horror of the Holocaust? Beethoven, Michelangelo, Leonardo da Vinci? I certainly felt inadequate and unqualified for such a task. Eventually I realized that if I didn't do it, someone else would. So I accepted.

After I finished, the editor asked if I would write an article about my own experience in the camps. That was very painful and hard to do. I wanted to express a feeling, rather than tell a story. I selected quotations from the Bible, which are carved on the walls in the Jewish Memorial Cemetery for the Martyrs in Budapest: "They were killed by hatred; their memory is kept alive in love." "I cried out against the brutality, but no one listened." "Even death could not come between us." "Even the stones weep."

When the October issue of *Minnesota Medicine* appeared, my Nordic colleagues at the University of Minnesota Hospital did not respond with the usual Swedish and Norwegian reserve. Many of them hugged me and cried.

A few weeks later the illustration appeared in the *Minneapolis Tribune* and Mrs. Candy Ames, an educator from Pine City, Minnesota, called and asked if I would give some lectures in her school. Although I had never even heard of Pine City, it became a turning point in my life.

On the first evening I talked to seven parents in a small library. I said that when the Nazis occupied Hungary, I was working in the country division of the Jewish Council. One day, a very excited man came to talk to the head of the division. His behavior was so unusual that I was curious and stayed inside the door after I let him in. He described the first loading of the Jews into boxcars: they were jammed shoulder-to-shoulder, squeezed together, without food or water, with only the clothes on their backs. The doors were locked from the outside, and the trains were heading toward an unknown destination.

When I heard about the brutality, it became clear to me that the Nazis wanted to kill us. This changed my attitude completely. Until then I was afraid of the air raids. Now I realized that either the Nazis would kill us or they would lose the war. From then on I wasn't afraid of the bombs. In fact, they made me euphoric. They brought me a step closer to my survival.

After my speech a gentleman stood up and said: "Doctor Fisch, I am so grateful to you." He was a bombardier over Budapest and had always felt guilty about killing innocent people. Now he saw that his actions also had another purpose. He had never told his family about his experience in the war. I later learned that he had finally opened up and talked to them.

The next day I talked to different classes. One student watched my speech very intently. When I finished, she stood up and said, "Dr. Fisch, I'm a visiting Danish student. I thank you very much for your speech. My grandparents saved a Jewish family, and now I know what that really meant."

After watching me in the classroom that day, Mrs. Ames said, "Your stories have such an impact on the students, why don't you write a book?"

So that's the way it happened.

I called the book: *Light from the Yellow Star; A Lesson of Love from the Holocaust*. A lesson of love? How can anyone suggest learning love from the Holocaust? By remembering not just the horror but also the beauty created by human virtue and enlightened by the suffering spirit. What would those silent millions ask of us now? To hate and to be unforgiving (the very qualities that led to their demise)? No, I believe they would want us to have understanding, compassion and love.

In 1994, with the help by the Yellow Star Foundation (established by my friend Erwin A. Kelen), the book was published. The response was overwhelming. The Yellow Star Foundation distributed the book free to schools, and it was selected as one of the best educational pieces in 1998 in the English Journal for English teachers in the United States.

I began getting more and more invitations to talk in different schools in Minnesota as well as in cities in the United States and Europe. Most audiences were students between 12 and 18 years of age, but I also spoke in colleges and universities and to adult audiences.

When I talk to students, I do not emphasize what the Nazis did with the Jews, but rather, how those events might apply to how students live and relate to others today. To be respected you have to respect others. Stand up for your principles, because compromise is the first step toward actions you eventually regret. The only change you can expect in this life is the change you are personally able to make. Young people growing up in the United States have an incredible opportunity. The future is in their hands, and they can go as far as they are able.

I began asking the students to write to me about their thoughts and feelings. The letters are not for grades, and the teachers mail them to me. I've received letters and drawings from 71 schools—from 49 teachers and 2101 students. Only two of the letters were negative, saying the writers did not want to hear about the past.

Talking to young people and reading their letters has become the most rewarding experience of my life—even more rewarding than medicine. To have a close relationship with a child (or family), a pediatrician has either to be with them from infancy through adulthood or take care of a chronic condition. In a class I spend two hours (an hour speaking and an hour taking questions) and can have an impact on someone for a lifetime. When I finished my talk in a New Jersey high school and asked if there were any questions, a 14-year-old girl stood up and asked, "Can I give you a hug?"

The young people of today are just as sensitive, curious and open to learning as at any other time. They are hungry to find their roles and relationships and moral values. Our role is not only to love, but also to teach moral and human values, to teach about love and compassion. They not only need it, they want it so very much.

I feel that if I can have an influence on one young person's life, then my time was well spent. And if I remain in only a single heart and mind, my life will have been worth living.

Dr. Robert O. Fisch
September 2003

I Met a Fish

I met a fish who swims dark water
And uses light to bait his hook.

"I dreamed of wire," he tells me gently
"And put it down in a picture book.

I speak in schools, I talk to children.
They send me letters that make me weep.

Some are afraid they'll become monsters
While others fear they'll be like sheep.

And I've seen both within my neighbors
And I've found both inside of me,

But when I fed a man I hated
It gave me strength and set me free."

I met a fish who swims dark water
And tries to help us find the light.

When dreams are dark he finds a window
And watches stars fill up the night.

—Kathleen Cleberg

Contents

1. Learning about the Holocaust

"You woke me up"

See more,
hear more,
read more,
learn more,
the mind has no boundary.

* The quotations following the chapter headings are taken from the letters. All other poems and remarks are by Doctor Fisch.

I speak in the name of those who cannot speak anymore, not to make a memento of the horror but to know it and to learn from it. Perhaps no medium is appropriate to describe the scope of the tragedy of the Holocaust. How can sorrow, suffering, and atrocities, and the death of six million people, be illustrated and appropriately expressed?

R. O. F.

You taught me that it was very hard to be Jewish during this time period. And how one person can make a big difference. And you who has informed many people of your experiences and taught them that one thing can change a person's whole life. You in the same sense have changed my whole life in some way by coming and talking to us. It just makes me a little more educated. It wasn't the easiest thing to come and talk to a bunch of rowdy eighth-graders about such a serious subject.

S. K., Cleveland Quality Middle School

We have been studying the Holocaust for a while now, and I have studied it before, but never in this depth. We have watched film footage of liberation of some concentration camps, we have read books, poetry, essays, but it was never real. When you came to speak to us, it all clicked for me. I started to realize that this really happened and it happened to real people.

G. F., South High School

You seemed to turn the nameless, faceless thing called Holocaust into a personal matter.

A. C., South High School

Your vast knowledge and insights on life left an everlasting impression on me. I learned many things about World War II and the Holocaust that I never knew before. It was an experience I will never forget.

R. O., Pulaski High School

We've been studying the Holocaust for a long time, but a real live survivor is amazing. Watching you up there, realizing you lived through it made me sick. You are a huge impact on me and many other people.

E. S., Roseville Area Middle School

Your personal recollections helped me understand the Holocaust and respect what happened. Your speech had such a greater impact than any history book or video.

K. W., Roseville Area Middle School

You woke me up. You were right when you said the Holocaust seems distant in both time and geography to us. Seeing and hearing your speech made me realize that the Holocaust shouldn't be buried, but used to prevent similar tragedies.

A. B., Ramsey Jr. High School

I find it interesting that we can learn so many dates and facts about the Holocaust and still miss the point. To have you here, in front of us, using your story as an example of the bigger picture, was an honor.

J. J., South High School

I can read all the facts and statistics, but what does that mean to me? It's just words on paper. Hearing your talk, someone who actually went through the hell I've read about, made it much more real to me.

I. H., South High School

I know statistics and stories, but listening to a survivor speak his experiences did something more than those. It showed me how real this past is. How awful and scary it is. But it also showed me how important it is to remember. Most of all, it opened my mind to avoid this from ever happening again.

E. B., South High School

2. Understanding the Loss

"...all those people were like you or me..."

Trees grow high,
birds can fly,
but only man can laugh and cry
at the same time.

They say that one man's death is a tragedy, a hundred
is a disaster, and a thousand is a statistic. The loss of
one person, even multiplied by six million, cannot be
measured in mathematical terms.

R. O. F.

I thought of the Holocaust as a tragic event that killed millions of people, that happened many years ago. I never thought of people in the Holocaust as individuals with their own story to tell. But now that I read poems and experiences written by Holocaust survivors, and listened to you speak, I know that everyone who experiences the Holocaust were people like anyone else. I learned that something like the Holocaust could happen to me, so now I try not to take life for granted, not focus on what I want and focus more on what I have.

M. R. S., South High School

You have taught me that you shouldn't stereotype anyone. You've taught me not to take revenge but of all things, you taught me it's not the number of people who die, it's who dies. There is a lot for you to teach and you're teaching people that hate isn't the way.

C. P., Cleveland Quality Middle School

When you told us at the beginning of class that you were a healer, not here to open up wounds but educate, it really grabbed my attention. I really started listening. It was such a different approach than most of the stories we've heard. Although our class learned all the facts and statistics, there's no way we could have learned about the more personal experiences other than through people like yourself. I think these things are far more important for us to learn than numbers.

M. L., South High School

I don't know anyone who went through anything like that or anyone who has died, but you showed me how personal it was. 6,000,000 is such a large number, but you showed me they were not a number, they were human.

A. S., Roseville Area Middle School

I know I'll think about you a lot because we always take life for granted, but I needed to hear about living day by day because you never know what could be next. I lost my father 5 yrs. ago in a car accident where someone ran a stop sign and he was killed instantly. You don't understand the loss of death until you yourself have gone through it. I just don't know how to thank you enough. Your words of wisdom and life were so powerful. You touched my heart in many ways.

J. B., Holdingford High School

There are hardly any words that I can write to show you how much you touched my life. Being "a person of color" and also of European descent, I too would have been put in a death camp. Not only that, but you put a face, a voice, to the many people who were persecuted, not just a mass of people I've seen on television. And the sad thing is that all those people were like you or me, with feeling and thoughts. Dr. Fisch, you are doing such a wonderful thing by speaking of your experiences, but also in your everyday job. I thank you with all my heart.

R. M. N., Roseville Area Middle School

I am never surprised by the number of people I am told have died, because it is impossible for me to think of them as individual humans. He said that did not matter, he helped me realize that the number really does not matter. What matters is that every one of the people that died was a mother, father, grandma, grandpa, aunt, uncle, brother, sister, cousin, to someone. Imagine how horrible you feel when you attend the funeral of a loved one. Try to multiply that but there is no funeral, no certainty that a person is dead or alive. Imagine everyone in your family dying. You are all alone.

Unsigned, South High School

You gave us many important messages to carry with us throughout our lives. The Holocaust is definitely a lesson in humility and love; one must never forget. I believe that your words will be remembered in our class until the last of us is gone, and that we will pass on the message to the next generation. I see if we do not do this, we put ourselves in danger of the same thing happening. As our class has studied the Holocaust, we have watched many videos and read many articles about the subject. However even the poetry we read, written by survivors, cannot be measured in terms of the emotion that filled the room as you spoke to us. For me your words came into me and touched me in the way that nothing I've experienced in school did before. When I heard you, I could feel pain and love, all rooted from the Holocaust. In a small way I felt what the Holocaust must have been like.

A. C., South High School

3. Seeing Prejudice and Hate

"the Beast is still there"

Dark...dark...dark...dark.
No present, no future, just the past
Dark, dark, no light, just dark.

Although we are individuals, we have more similarities than differences. The bell-shaped curve applies to every human circumstance. No religion, nation, or race is exempt from the fact that a small extreme exists on each side of the curve, and the rest of us are in the center.

R. O. F.

You taught me that instead of fighting, we should group together to try to overcome the problem. We shouldn't put labels on others based on Race, Religion, gender, age, etc. I thought that it was very interesting that a person who went though so much could be so calm.

J., South High School

I have now realized that hatred can do so much damage, and that no one should have hatred in them. I was very surprised when you said that you have no hatred in you - especially after what happened to you. That just really shows what a caring person you are. You have really inspired me to be a better person.

K. T., Central Middle School

I think about how cruel human beings can be to one another. I can't say 'never be mean' because that would not be realistic, but the 10 commandments would never be broken. There are so many stubborn people in this world who really need to wake up and learn that if you cannot say anything nice, don't say anything at all.

D. S., St. Croix Valley Alternative Learning Program

I learned how to treat people better. What I learned most is not to seek revenge. Like when you had the chance to kick that poor German beggar, but instead you helped him. I also learned to not be mean to people who are different than me, no matter how other people treat them. People are people and that's all there is to it.

R. M., Orono Middle School

I learned that only a few wicked people can kill a few million innocents. I find it very hard to believe that the Holocaust actually happened. It is too horrible to visualize and I feel very sorry for the people and the families of the people who died. I think one lesson we can learn is how to prevent it from happening again. It is so unfair that people are discriminated against because of their race, religion or color.

A. M., Orono Middle School

We are pupils of the local school at Gunnskirchen (Austria). Most of us were born in 1981. This means we have grown up in a time of prosperity and peace. Nevertheless, it is very important to us to tell you, what we, as representatives of the Austrian youth, think about the events 50 years ago. We are only 14 years old and the grown-ups and voters of tomorrow. About one topic we agree: We want to try everything that we can to ensure that something like that never happens again.

A letter for the 50th anniversary by students in Gunskirchen, Austria

Always my emotions have been that of sorrow and guilt for those who suffered. My feelings have changed when I read on the first page "It is not the ugliness of hate but the beauty of love which survives in time." I will always be sad for what was lost in our past, but through this quote, and through the strength bluntly stated in your paintings, I find the most important thing to do is to celebrate the love and life of those whose lives were lost and through the experience learn to not repeat history.

L. H., South High School

We need to be aware of what happened so we can recognize the patterns in events. Because "the Beast is still here." Racism, intolerance and violence are always around us.

M. D., University of St. Thomas

4. Responding to the Art

"You spoke to me through your art"

Thinking is for individuals.
Communication is for all of us.

In my art I use barbed wire to illustrate ghettos, concentration camps, isolation. The shred of the yellow star represents loneliness, the loss of dignity, the branding of a tatoo. Red signifies the existence of horror, torture, suffering, bleeding. Black symbolizes hopelessness, despair, and death. Each line, form and color is a different shade of sorrow.

R. O. F.

The way you used hands in your paintings was really neat because they each represented something.

M. M., Our Lady of Grace

Take people to the light, out of the dark. Give these bony hands food, show love to brother kind.

E. A., Burnsville High School

I first saw a hand that looked red and black and that was it. It didn't really hit me until I read the story, then I saw death, pain, suffering, and the truth.

M. S., Burnsville High School

I think my favorite picture in your book is the peasant handing someone an apple. I like your explanation of this painting, that her hand is proportionate to the apple and the others are not. I also like the last picture of all the color and the darkness slowly fades away.

R., Pulaski High School

My favorite painting is the one with the face in black. I think that painting best describes how alone you must have been and how isolated you felt.

A., Orono Middle School

One of the pictures that sticks with me is the "1" with big numbers inside of it. It is so true what you said about comprehending the numbers involved with death. One death is just as painful as many when a person loses a loved one.

A. G., Sauk Center

I am a student of art and I thought your paintings were wonderful. And I can't explain to you how much they magnified your lecture; they give a frighteningly powerful focal point that helped me visualize your words.

G. S., Central High School

Your paintings explained things that words never could.

K. G., Robbinsdale High School

Never before have I seen these experiences expressed. When someone speaks of the things they faced you hear mostly how it affected them and how they reacted. But when I saw your paintings, I saw what you saw. And in the colors, the strokes, the symbols, I saw what you felt.

B. L., South High School

I really loved the simplicity of color and that there were so few of them used. It made them very striking and all meaningful. They all got me to look at the Holocaust in a slightly different way. There were two in particular that really moved me and I found myself thinking about them afterwards. "I heard the news: I trembled and became speechless" was almost too much to bear - something about the red smoke and the reaching hands. The other was each person who died in the Holocaust was a *person* and not just a number. A person with family, hopes, dreams, and people who loved them. I think that it is the hardest thing to fully realize. Every person was an individual: each life lost was a life lost. That picture was one of the things that showed the relationship between the victim of the Holocaust and a survivor. Just one of the millions that existed. It changed my view of the Holocaust as a whole. Without bringing down the horribleness of its occurrence, it also helped shed a new light on it. It meant a lot to me. I will remember your visit for a long time to come.

S. J. W., South High School

5. Finding the Positive

"Dr. Fisch still has sunshine in his heart"

Our fear was vanished
Our hope became reality
Our dream will be the future.

As beautiful pearls are produced by the suffering of an oyster, so the Holocaust created beautiful heroes—not only among the victims and survivors but also among those who risked their lives to help and save the persecuted. The Holocaust teaches us that love overcomes hate. Suffering and deprivation can make us value the basic essentials of living. Every minute of my life is a gift.

R. O. F.

One thing I learned from your presentation is that, even after such a traumatic experience, you can still be kind and generous.

R. A., Cleveland Quality Middle School

Now that I have heard your stories, I feel I know what you went through but I find that I will never really know the pain and agony every Jew faced. I was intrigued by your presentation, and I admire how you show that life must go on. I've known this before, but you really helped to show me that we must live life to the fullest. We must find the good things in life, and always keep positive. I believe this is the message for everyone. I cannot tell you how much your speaking to us meant to me.

B. S., South High School

I think the first lesson was that you had to hang in there. A second lesson (like the lesson of love) was that you had to remember the good times, you also had to remember that God is by your side, and no matter what, you had to remember that you can get through anything.

H. S., Orono Middle School

It must take an enormous heart to achieve the level of peace you seem to have about this. I know anger & thirst for vengeance are natural, but to overcome these takes much greater courage and understanding. Yours was a testament to hope and love.

L. A., Central High School

You must have suffered more than I or anyone else could ever imagine. And nevertheless, you didn't only write about the cruelty and hopelessness. You wrote about the German soldiers who felt pity for you and the others and gave you food, and about the woman who risked her life only to give an apple to the poor suffering people. You saw a little humanity within the horrors of war.

K. T., Hildburghausen Germany

I have heard Holocaust survivors speak before, but I never heard them speak about moving on and not holding grudges against the German people. This thought of moving on and not dwelling on how you were so horribly wronged, seems to be a healthy attitude to hold. Being Jewish myself, I found your view especially amazing.

D. K., South High School

You showed me not only the negative sides, but that there is a way to change this terrible time into a positive impression too. Everyone knows that it was horrible and I know cruel details, but you noticed also some positive gestures and you learned to overcome the bad experiences and not to hate everybody. I get the impression that what you learned during that time was to love.

E. H., Klagenfurt Germany

I'm glad you're letting others benefit from your horrible experience. Love does overcome hate.

C. B., Roseville Area Middle School

You were able to emerge from your experience with love. Though there was so much hate and destruction, you were able to show your audience love and compassion. It really amazed me that you spoke of not wanting revenge or to be a judge or feeling overcome by hatred. I admire your desire to teach others to live with people and not against them.

E. L., South High School

6. Having Character

"Not budging in what you believe"

Our priority should be to build children's character.

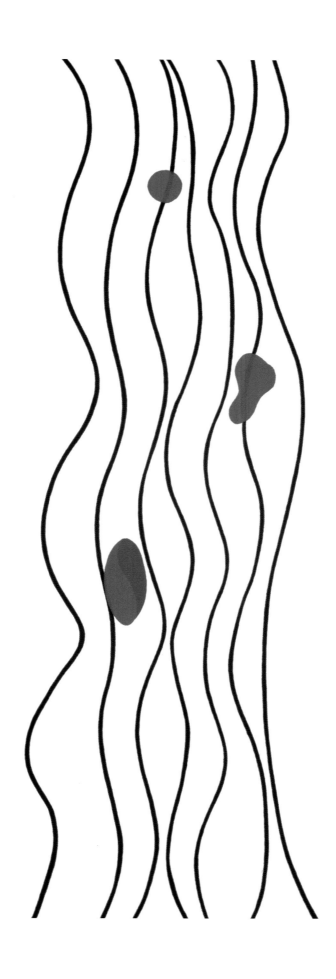

I have a special obligation to show that my life is more than survival. The most important lesson I have learned is that we must always remain human, toward everyone, in all circumstances, however brutal. We are born neither good nor bad. We don't inherit our parents' values and morals. Each generation has to learn anew how to be civilized. In the face of tyranny and injustice, we have to stand up and fight.

R.O.F.

You said so many things that I never want to forget. One of them was, "In this world the only change can be done by you. Don't rely on others to do it."

A. J., Central Middle School

After we heard your message I think we value life even more. I really liked your message about standing up for who you are and to fight for your rights.

C. P., Ogilvie High School

So many people say that something like the Holocaust could never happen again, will never happen again. But look at how easily it happened before. Education is the key to clarity and peace and by educating my class about the Holocaust, there are 50 more people willing to fight back against discrimination.

K. H. R., South High School

You said a hungry German asked you for food and that was a turning point for you. You did give him food, which I think is a wonderful thing. I'd like to think I would do the same, but I don't know. You said, basically, one must distinguish between Right and Wrong.

M. G., Central Middle School

You said things that I can use for life and not just for history class. For example, you told us to live our lives and not let others take our beliefs away from us.

A. G., Sauk Center High School

Would I have the strength you had? Or would I give up like so many did. Your speech was so heart-warming, I took all I learned that morning and shared it with my family. I will treasure your words.

K. K., Orono Middle School, Orono MN

I find it completely amazing that you have no resentments or hatred toward anyone. I also liked how you told us to stand up for yourself, no matter what is happening.

B. Z., Sauk Center High School

I like the underlying message of kindness, humanity and not budging in what you believe in.

C. M., Roseville Area Middle School

I think it's really important for kids to know about the Holocaust and, by telling us, you're helping to get the right message into our heads so that hopefully, when it's our turn to make decisions, we'll make the right ones.

C., Ramsey Jr. High School

You delivered a positive talk in which you challenged us to prevent another Holocaust from occurring in the future.

C. H., South High School

I realize that it is my duty to become an active member of the citizens of the world and promote good relations.

C. R., South High School

This new level of thinking raises my level of disgust and horror, that humankind could ever commit such atrocities. However, it is necessary for me to feel this way so that, if the time ever comes for me to stand up for or against a people or their actions, I will have learned and felt something about the past and have a reference point from which to make my stand.

M. T., South High School

7. Appreciating Freedom

"I use every moment I can"

Not just certain days,
but every day is special.

Freedom brings responsibilities as well as rights. You who were born free and have the opportunity to fulfill your heart's desire are among the rarest group in the history of mankind. Those who are free must guard their freedom and extend it to those who are less fortunate.

R. O. F.

"You are the only one who can forgive. There is no representation in forgiveness." It really makes you stand out as an individual. Your greatest effect on me has been allowing myself to take advantage of every moment of my freedom. I understand that it could be stripped from me any time, it happened to you, so I use every moment I can.

K. M., South High School

I myself am a Jewish girl. When I see survivors or hear about the Holocaust, it makes me feel very grateful that I was born two generations later.

S. L., Ramsey Junior High School

I learned a lot from you, not just about the Holocaust, but about life. I am going to try to be appreciative and not take things for granted.

J. S., Roseville Area Middle School

People my age don't realize how lucky we are to be where we are and to have freedom. It is difficult to appreciate something until it is taken away from you. What I got out of this was a greater understanding of the Holocaust and greater appreciation for my own life and privileges.

L. W., South High School

I learned from you that, even in the worst moments, there's always some type of humanity, that we have to appreciate our freedom and finally, that we should never do anything we would not like to happen to us.

G. G., St. Louis Park High School

Some of the things you said made me realize how lucky I really am and that several things, including life itself, should not be taken for granted.

T. T., South High School

I have learned that you should enjoy life as it is and not take it for granted. Because you never know what's coming your way. Life is very great!! We, here in America, have some things people never have had: FREEDOM; to like who ever we want, do whatever we want to do and stand up for our rights.

E. P., St. Louis Park High School

Thanks to you, I see history differently - I see my life differently. Things I take for granted every single day have taken on brilliant colors.

C. M., South High School

You really reminded me just how lucky we are to be free and (as we grow up in this nation), how much we take for granted. It is very good to have a reminder once in a while and I will try to be more appreciative and not complain about petty things so much. I learned a lot from your speech.

E. G., Wayzata West

I can honestly say I believe your talk changed my life in a way. When you talked about freedom and enjoying simple things in life (like a baked potato), it made me step back and look at my own life. I do take way too much for granted, and sometimes I feel like I let things pass me without fully noticing them. Hearing your talk about how it truly is a gift just to be alive and able to experience things has made me try to just stop and look around a bit more.

S. J. W., South High School

One student asked Dr. Fisch what was the most important thing he taught that we should remember. One of his answers was to be thankful for life and grateful for every moment. I've heard people say that, but coming from him it had more effect. I will never forget what he said.

G. H., South High School

8. Empathy

"How painful this must be for you"

The nights are long,
but life is short.

I have tried to give the illusion that you are walking with me in the Jewish Memorial Cemetery for the Martyrs in Budapest, where my father is buried. I want to share how I feel when I walk among those weeping gravestones—in reality and in my dreams.

R. O. F.

I think that it would be very hard to survive and have enough guts to come here and talk about it. What fascinated me was that you survived and you were able to feed that hungry German.

J. M., Cleveland Quality School

Even though the Holocaust is a painful part of your past (of everyone's past), talking about it is the only way it will be prevented from happening again.

D. K., South High School

Thank you for giving us your input and how you survived The Living Hell. Well, I hope the rest of your days end with peace.

T. C., Cleveland Quality School

I know it must have been hard for you to relive this traumatic experience but it must be told to us so we won't make the same *horrible* mistake.

C. M., Roseville Area Middle School

Your talk was fascinating and it was so kind of you to relive those horrible times in your life for our benefit.

Unsigned, Roseville Area Middle School

It must be hard for you to discuss the Holocaust, with so many people dying, including your father. It's a good thing that you didn't go to what they called a "hospital," otherwise you wouldn't be here to tell us and share with us your sad and amazing story.

M. B., Our Lady of Grace

You have a lot of courage to come and talk about something that left a hole in your heart for the rest of your life.

Z. B., Roseville Area Middle School

We understand how painful this must be for you, so this talk was very touching for all of us.

W. R. P., Roseville Area Middle School

I know that it was hard to share such information that usually no one can share. Meeting you was a once in a lifetime chance and it was great.

S. S. P., Battle Creek Middle School

I think you are very brave to be able to speak about your horrible past and to "relive" the Holocaust.

Unsigned, Fred Moore Middle School

9. Sympathy and Condolences

"I feel very sorry for you and your family"

To remain in only a single heart and mind,
my life will have been worth living.

The death of my father was the death of the world as I had known it. He always gave to others; he gave his food to the needier ones and he starved to death. Before he died, he said that if one man can do this to another, there was no reason for him to go back. He was so highly respected in the camp that he was the only one not buried in a common grave. We brought him back, and he was the first to be buried in the Jewish Memorial Cemetery for the Martyrs in Budapest.

R.O.F.

The story I like the most is, "I cried out against the brutality, but nobody listened." I don't understand why they tore up pictures of your loved ones, that would hurt me more than any abuse and it would leave the biggest scar.

K. H., Cleveland Quality School

I wish I could know for just one minute what exactly you went though. I know my words probably don't mean a whole lot to you or bring you much comfort, but I'm sorry about everything that's happened, especially the death of your father. You have touched my life in a way nobody else has. Thank you.

J. S., Central Middle School

I'm feel sorry for what happened to you and I hope you feel better (pretend that you're a butterfly. It might make you feel better).

C., Homecraft Elementary

One part of your story was extra sad. That was the part when you told us about your father. Your father sounded like a great man and I am sorry he died, but I am glad you did not die. I cannot fully express my feelings about your story, but I wanted you to know that your story was extremely sad and really moved me.

J. B., Our Lady of Grace

I am sorry that anything had to happen to you and your family to make me (and others) understand what a human life means and why we should always be human.

Unsigned, Central High School

It just took my breath away to hear what the Germans did to you and your family. I am very sorry for your losses, but you sure turned out to be a great guy!

A. H., Holdingforth High School

I know that I could never be able to experience what you went through. It is a horrible tragic incident and I'm very mournful toward you because of your father.

J. M. F., Fred Moore Middle School

Dr. Fisch talked about a person and held up a picture, at the camp, a number of years later. She was still looking for her father. My emotions just hit me then. It was hard when Dr. Fisch was talking to keep my emotions under control. At some points in his speech I wanted to cry or give the man a hug. He has lived through so much it's unimaginable.

A. A., Burnsville High School Senior Campus

10. Gratitude for Coming

"This was so inspiring"

*Kindness and friendship
are the greatest gifts.*

As a doctor my role is healing. I want to spread the principles of belief that will create a good quality of life, with self-respect and respect for and by others. Don't expect the world to change. The only change is that which you can make, and then you might be able to change others.

R. O. F.

It is wonderful to hear people of your generation encouraging and believing in mine. It helps us believe in ourselves, helping us to learn who we are in order to develop our own morals and values which we are not afraid to stand up for. I've found the warmth and strength of others helps to bring out your own. Your visit was extremely enlightening and encouraging.

V. W., South High School

It affected me that you came not just to tell us your story, but also to make our lives better through your wisdom.

L. C., South High School

Thank you for coming to our school to teach us about the Holocaust. There are not enough people out there to teach good things to the young minds. p.s. You are the most forgiving person I've seen.

J. V., Cleveland Middle School

I really think you should come next year because my sister and more generations need this talk to take in and be left with an imprint like you made on me, Dr. Fisch. The part where you said that your father gave up his food and how soldiers gave you some meager extras. This was so inspiring.

M. T., Central Middle School

It's like the Holocaust filled a cup up with sludge, but Dr. Fisch is pouring out purified water. Not every bad thing should stay bad. We should learn something good and meaningful with it.

I. P., South High School

I bet it's hard to go back to all those terrible memories and talk about it to total strangers. But we really appreciate it and it helps other people to create a better idea of what really happened.

T. T., South High School

My Friend, Thank You

My Friend I wish you could know
how much your words have spoken
The strongest wings are those that
have been Bound.
Being bound by something can help us grow
until the day we are able to break
through, and show that we are who we are.
Like a caterpillar, we hold something
special inside, we hide it, until the
day we can break through, turn into a butterfly.
Sometimes this is physical,
like loss of sight or hearing,
or mental, unable to read,
loss of self esteem,
but you, you were
locked into a Ghetto,
burned in concentration camps.
Tortured at the hands of Nazis.
But you spoke. You drew.
You sang. And you
forgave. Your life
may have been brief,
but you left an imprint in
time. You showed us
love, in a time when
hate dominated our
world, and we will never forget.
Thank you for breaking
your bonds. Thank you for
living your life. Thank you for
your hope. Thank you.

Brittany Knudson, Central Middle School

11. Admiration and Affection

"P. S. I love your accent!"

Valuables are not what you leave in the bank,
but your place in human hearts and minds.

We survivors have a special obligation. I did not become judge, even though I was a victim. Now I have to show that my life is more than survival. When I reach the end of my days and make inventory of my actions, I want to be able to say that I did the right thing for myself and for others, that my time was spent well and my life was valuable and worthwhile.

R. O. F.

I would like to tell you that the day you visited was the most interesting day of school I've ever had. I spent the next two days thinking about the things you said.

H. Z., South High School

Never in my life have I watched a presenter speak on such an emotional issue with such sensitivity and good will. You are truly an inspiration of hard work and courage.

J. H., Pine City High School

You have my respect and, I hope, everyone else's. You are one great man, but in my eyes a hero.

K. O. H., Pine City High School

If I were a guard back then I would have risked my life to help you escape if I knew how nice of a man you were.

M. P., Roseville Area Middle School

The book you wrote was beautiful, it touched my heart, and having you come and talk about the Holocaust. You are a Hero to me. I will always remember the day you came.

A. T., Our Lady of Grace

You just blew me away. I thought that a Holocaust survivor would be bitter and angry, but you are not. I don't know if I could be that way in your position. I think you are an example for everyone.

L. J. S., South High School

I am so incredibly *proud* of you. You deserve many applauses. You are sincerely a strong person—both emotionally and physically. I am deeply troubled by the way you and other Jews were persecuted and treated. I am sorry your precious father did not survive. I read your outstanding book and I was truly amazed. Your art work is full of sorrow and endless pain, yet it is so incredibly symbolic. We all must be educated about the past so this kind of thing does not happen again. How could you survive through those horrid conditions? How could *anyone*? I know you still carry those painful memories of brutality and that there is a deep agony in your inner self, therefore, I appreciate you so much for speaking to our class to share your mortifying experiences. You highly educated me and my fellow classmates that day. To imagine you becoming a physician and an accomplished artist after what had happened to you is fascinating. I acknowledge all of the symbolic meanings in your sorrowful artwork and writing. You are a courageous and deep person who can express your pain and suffering through symbols in your artwork and writings. This is a truly great quality of yours. Your occupation also greatly benefits society. Once again, I sincerely thank you so much for opening up to us in sharing your harsh experiences. You will always be remembered. You are also a HERO in my book!!

M. D., Fridley High School

All I can say is thanks (heart drowning) for talking (heart drowning), for being you; thanks (heart drowning) for living out your world! (heart drowning). P.S. I love your accent!

K. B., Holdingford High School

The past is the past
Victims and their murderers have all become dust
Only justice is left.

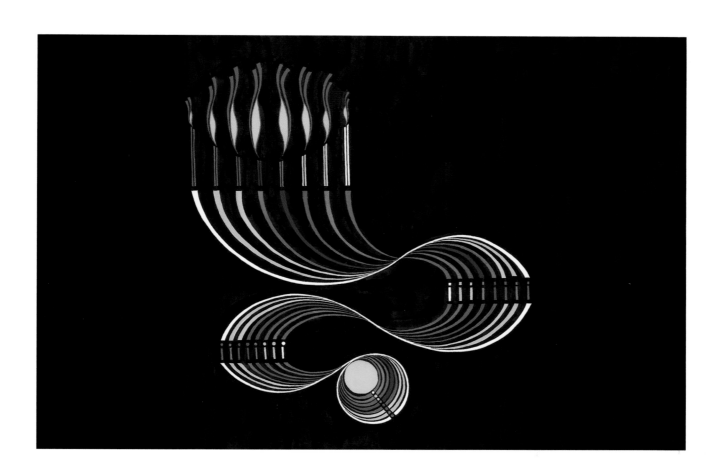

Epilogue

As I read through an overwhelming number of letters and responses, I realized the students were doing more than responding to a presentation. They were sending messages of their own. Telling us who they are, how they see the world, what they're afraid of, whom they admire, and what they want to become.

What did Dr. Fisch expect when he stepped in front of that first class? Was he hoping the students would show moderate attention? Was he fearing they would talk through his presentation or sleep at their desks?

I know he did not expect what happened in that classroom and in every classroom he's entered since. He could not imagine the students would be so grateful for his efforts that they'd try to give him something back. That they stand up to hug him and open their hearts to him in healing words and drawings.

In letter after letter, the children speak honestly about emotions that most adults are afraid to show. Who but a child would offer condolences to a Holocaust survivor as if it all happened yesterday? Who but a child would say "Pretend that you're a butterfly, it might make you feel better."

By taking the time to talk to them and by reliving the horrors of his past, Dr. Fisch is telling kids he's never met that he respects them and cares for them. In return, these kids are telling a man they just met that his message has changed their lives. In this quiet moment the wisdom and strength of age meets the idealism and enthusiasm of youth and creates a beautiful example of the power of love.

Kathleen Cleberg
September 2003

The Yellow Star Foundation
http://www.yellowstarfoundation.org

The Yellow Star Foundation is a not-for-profit organization dedicated to helping educate young people about the Holocaust using Dr. Robert Fisch's book, *Light From the Yellow Star - A Lesson of Love from the Holocaust.*

Because of the enthusiastic reception to Dr. Fisch's many personal classroom presentations, the Foundation recently completed a video that brings the experience of a visit from Dr. Fisch into every classroom. The video has four ten-minute sections and includes Dr. Fisch's background, his experiences during World War II, his work as both a doctor and an artist, his classroom presentations and student response.

The Yellow Star Foundation website (yellowstarfoundation.org) builds on the great success of Dr. Robert Fisch to teach junior high school and high school students about the Holocaust. The Yellow Star Foundation website includes lesson plans, video clips, a teachers' forum, classroom ideas, links to resources (books, videos, and web sites), classroom dos and don'ts, information about the Holocaust, and profiles of projects successfully used in other parts of the country.

The Foundation raises money from individuals and foundations to print and distribute the book and video to schools, relying on all-volunteer help.

YELLOW STAR FOUNDATION
c/o Kelen Ventures
One Financial Plaza, Suite 2005
120 South Sixth Street
Minneapolis, MN 55402
erwin@kelenventures.com

"Cause when you're prejudiced to one you're prejudiced to all."
—from a student's letter to Dr. Fisch